WINDOWS OF TRUTH

Peter Jeffery

Illustrated by
Lawrence Littleton Evans

D1350479

THE BANNER OF TRUTH TRUST

THE BANNER OF TRUTH TRUST
3 Murrayfield Road, Edinburgh EH12 6EL
PO Box 621, Carlisle, Pennsylvania 17013, USA

★

© Peter Jeffery 1992
First published 1992
ISBN 0 85151 636 X

★

Typeset in 10½ on 12 pt Plantin by
Smallprint, Haywards Heath, West Sussex
Printed in Great Britain by
Courier International Limited
East Kilbride, Scotland

Contents

Introduction

The Bible is a book that makes full use of simple but vivid illustrations to help make its message clear. In the early chapters of Genesis, sin is illustrated as 'crouching at your door; it desires to have you, but you must master it' (Gen. 4:7). Sin is like a wild animal waiting to pounce on its unsuspecting prey.

The prophet Hosea is commanded by God to marry the prostitute Gomer so that his life with her can serve as an illustration of the way God's people treat God (Hos. 1:2). Gomer is unfaithful to Hosea. She is sold into slavery and her husband has to buy her freedom. All this is a vivid illustration of Israel's unfaithfulness to God, her bondage to sin, and redemption through the love and grace of God.

Illustrations are not the same as parables. The parable can often be long, involved and not so easy to interpret. When Jesus told the parable of the seeds, the disciples, let alone the general crowd of people, could not understand it and had to have an interpretation from him. On the other hand, when Jesus used an illustration it was mostly brief, simple and clear. For instance, when he said, 'I am the door' (John 10:7), it clearly meant that no-one could enter the presence of God except through the Lord Jesus Christ.

It is not surprising, therefore, that preachers of the gospel follow this biblical example and use illustrations in their sermons. An illustration may be taken from the scriptures or from everyday events, but the purpose is to make clear a biblical truth. The illustration is not meant as light relief in the sermon; it is, said Spurgeon, to be a feather for an arrow, so that gospel truth may penetrate the human heart and mind.

Sadly, some preachers use too many illustrations and

the sermon then lacks biblical content. Spurgeon likened illustrations to windows in a home — they let in light. But he warned that too many windows would weaken the structure of the house. Some illustrations can just be tear-jerking stories told to create an emotional reaction. This is misuse of a valid biblical method. It is true that often the illustration is remembered long after the sermon is forgotten. This is not necessarily a bad thing if the illustration was good and what it intended to illustrate is also remembered.

A good illustration is short and sharp and clearly highlights the truth to which it is pointing. Its inclusion in the sermon is valid only if it illuminates biblical truth in a way that will rivet this truth upon the human mind and heart. Good illustrations are found not in books and other writings but in life itself. If a preacher wants illustrations, he needs to be continually thinking of the people to whom he is to preach, and to see in everyday things illustrations that will make God's eternal truth clear and relevant for these people.

This book is not for preachers. It is meant to put sermon illustrations in print and through them encourage God's people and convict those who are unbelievers by bringing to everyone basic Bible truths. It is meant to be a window of truth.

1: Pros Kairon

Bala in North Wales is a very Welsh town. The language spoken in the homes and shops is Welsh, and the names on the houses are, with very few exceptions, Welsh. One of these exceptions is the name-plate on a house that is passed if you enter the town on the Dolgellau road. The name is *Pros Kairon*. It is not Welsh, but Greek, and means 'for a while'.

Whoever gave the name to the house had wisdom and understanding. He knew that no home is permanent in this world. The house may stand for a hundred years or more, but we are here only for a while.

Here is a salutary reminder of a basic biblical truth. Life for us in this world is temporary, yet as creatures made in the image of God with immortal souls, life can be eternal.

2: See You Later

The Australians are famous for the unique way they say, 'Good day'. Another expression with a meaning almost unique to the Australian is, 'See you later'. This is a warm, friendly way of saying goodbye. It may or may not have any relevance to actual reality, suggesting that a future meeting is planned. I remember a few years ago, after preaching in a church in Sydney, standing at the door afterwards to shake hands with the people. So many said to me, 'See you later', that I began seriously to wonder if another meeting had been arranged for later that evening which no-one had told me about. But there was no extra meeting; it was just their friendly way of saying goodnight.

God says to us all, 'I will see you later'. He says this not only to Christians but to atheists, humanists and all sorts of unbelievers. The message of the gospel clearly reminds us that we are to see God later. And this is no friendly, harmless nicety but the serious warning that we must all one day meet God.

The gospel says, 'man is destined to die once, and after that to face judgment' (Heb. 9:27) and, 'we will all stand before God's judgment seat' (Rom. 14:10).

Jesus told a story to illustrate the Day of Judgment — 'All the nations will be gathered before him, and he will separate the people one from another as a shepherd separates the sheep from the goats. He will put the sheep on his right and the goats on his left. Then the King will say to those on his right, "Come, you who are blessed by my Father; take your inheritance, the kingdom prepared for you since the creation of the world" ' (Matt. 25:32-34). 'Then he will say to those on his left, "Depart from me, you who are cursed, into the eternal fire prepared for the devil and his angels. For I was hungry and you gave me nothing to eat, I was thirsty and you gave me nothing to drink, I was a stranger and you did not invite me in, I needed clothes and you did not clothe me, I was sick and in prison and you did not look after me" ' (Matt. 25:41-43).

'They also will answer, "Lord, when did we see you hungry or thirsty or a stranger or needing clothes or sick or in prison, and did not help you?" He will reply, "I tell you the truth, whatever you did not do for one of the least of these, you did not do for me." Then they will go away to eternal punishment, but the righteous to eternal life' (Matt. 25:44-46).

Yes, God will see us later. Are you looking forward to that meeting?

3: The Radar Trap

The coach sped down the road carrying its passengers on their day trip to the seaside. The driver chatted to those sitting near the front, pointing out interesting landmarks. After a while it was noticed that the drivers of lorries and coaches coming towards us were giving our driver the thumbs-down sign.

He knew what it meant. There was a police radar speed trap ahead, so he noticeably slowed down.

Sure enough, we soon saw a policeman standing at the roadside with a radar gun in his hand. We passed him well within the speed limit. As soon as we were past, our speed increased and our driver began to give the thumbs-down sign to lorries and coaches coming towards him.

The policeman would not have caught many law-

breakers that day. The law was politely adhered to only for as long as necessary and in effect the law-enforcer was laughed at.

There is a law and a law-enforcer who is not so easily fooled. God's law may be broken a thousand times by man, but he is never fooled. The Bible calls breaking God's law 'sin', and God declares most positively, 'be sure that your sin will find you out' (Num. 32:23).

There is a day of reckoning coming when we must all give an account for our sin to the divine law-enforcer. What fools we are to think that we can trick the omniscient God! He sees all and knows all. No sin is hidden from his sovereign eye. But thank God that he is not only the law-enforcer, but also a God of great mercy and grace who will pardon all our sin when we come to him in repentance and faith.

4: The Worst Way To Die

The teenagers from the church had gone back to the pastor's house as usual after the Sunday evening service. When the pastor arrived later, the boys were engrossed in a serious discussion on what was the worst way to die.

They had come up with a list of most painful deaths:

> eaten by a crocodile;
> run over by a steam-roller;
> boiled in oil.

The list was long and gruesome.

When the pastor came in, they asked his opinion. He answered them simply, the worst way to die is Christ-less.

The means by which any of us die is unimportant compared to the spiritual state we are in when we die. There are only two spiritual states: with Christ as our Saviour, or Christ-less.

The Bible says there are two deaths: the first death and the second death. The first death is the death of the body, and all — Christians and non-Christians alike — experience this. But the second death, which is hell (Rev. 20:14), the Christian is spared because his sin, which deserves hell, has been dealt with by his Saviour on the cross of Calvary.

How will you die — with or without the Lord Jesus Christ as your Saviour?

5: Whitewash

'Because they lead my people astray, saying, "Peace", when there is no peace, and because, when a flimsy wall is built, they cover it with whitewash' (Ezek. 13:10).

In Ezekiel 13 God is exposing false teachers who lead people astray with wrong teaching that gives men and women a false sense of security. They do a whitewash job, because they always bypass the question of God's holiness and man's sin.

God uses a picture of people building a wall —probably the city's wall to protect against an enemy. They build flimsy walls, that is, walls easy to erect, cheaply and quickly, but useless. The builders know this, but they cover up the deficiencies of their work with whitewash. This makes it look attractive, but it is still useless and God says it will fall.

Today people are encouraged to build flimsy walls of their own self-righteousness. Easy religion and senti-mental doctrine are popular. There must always be a feeling of well-being and so sin and hell are never mentioned. People think of the church as some sort of emotional aspirin to make them feel good.

It is all whitewash. It is a refusal to face the reality of the situation that the way people are building their lives is flimsy and unacceptable to almighty God.

How do we whitewash our lives? By trusting our own goodness and efforts; by comparing ourselves with others and concluding that we are better than they are, therefore we are O.K.

All this is the age-old doctrine of salvation by works, which the New Testament vigorously denounces. But if you accept it, then it is inevitable that you will reject the true gospel call for repentance. How many whitewashed souls there are! They look nice and respectable, and probably are, but their sinful hearts remain unchanged. Jesus likened them to white tombs — outside white and sparkling, but inside full of dead men's bones.

What is God's answer to whitewash? When I was a boy, I lived the first ten years of my life in a decaying old terraced house. We had two rooms upstairs and two down, but could only use one up and one down because the other two were too damp. The back yard was about three metres square, with high walls all around. The walls, like the house, were crumbling and decaying. To keep the back looking tidy, the walls had to be whitewashed every year. When it was done it looked lovely, but we knew it only covered up the decaying walls.

That went on for years; then the local council condemned the house and moved us into a new house. After that, there was no need for whitewash.

Is that not like many lives? They are spiritually decaying and crumbling. God says, 'I condemn that life. In my eyes it is foul and polluted with sin, and no amount of moral or religious whitewash will change it.' That is terrible, but the message of the gospel is that the God who condemns is also willing to move us out and provide a new life for us in the Lord Jesus Christ.

He is a God who does not whitewash, but blood-wash. He deals with our sin, laying it upon Jesus and allowing the Saviour to bear not only our sin and guilt, but also the punishment due to it. He died on the cross in our place to purchase for us a full and free salvation.

The Bible tells us that the blood of Jesus Christ alone can cleanse us from sin.

6: Lifeguards

If, on a hot summer's day, you were sitting in a deck-chair on the beach, and someone told you that particular beach had the best team of lifeguards in the country, you would not disbelieve them, but neither would you get too excited about the fact.

On the other hand, if you were half a mile out in the sea, with cramp in both legs and in great danger of drowning, and the same message was given to you, your reaction would be totally different. You would shout in desperation for those lifeguards to come to your assistance.

In both situations the message is the same, but your reaction is different. Why? Because, though in the deck-chair you do not doubt the truth about the lifeguards, you have no need of them. Out in the sea your situation is serious. You believe now with a desperate urgency. You need these lifeguards and you call passionately for their help.

Your reaction to the truth is governed by an awareness of your need. The same is true in our reaction to the gospel. You can listen to the gospel for years and, though you never doubt its truth, it just bounces off you like a rubber ball off a brick wall. It makes no impression whatsoever. But when you are convicted of sin and see yourself as a hell-deserving sinner under the wrath of the holy God, then the gospel message of forgiveness of sin and salvation in the Lord Jesus Christ becomes the most urgent and relevant thing you have ever heard. You cry in repentance for mercy.

Conviction of sin is absolutely essential to salvation. The degree of conviction will vary from one person to another, but it must be there. It is only those who know they are lost who will seek to be saved.

7: The Multi-Storey Car Park

Several years ago I was preaching on a Saturday night in the Colston Hall in Bristol, at the annual meeting of the West of England Festival of Male Voice Praise. The hall was packed with 2,000 people and after the meeting these spilled out onto the road to their cars and coaches. At the same time thousands more were leaving cinemas and theatres. The result was that the roads around Colston Hall were packed solid with traffic. Nothing was moving. It was a solid traffic jam.

We were parked in a multi-storey car park behind the hall, on the fifth floor of the eleven-storey building. All the ramps leading down to the road were filled bumper to bumper with cars. I thought we would never get out. One of my friends with me knew Bristol well, and he advised us not to go down as everyone else was doing, but to go up because there was an exit on the eighth floor. We did not believe this. It sounded impossible. How could you get out of a multi-storey car park on the eighth floor? But there was nothing to lose, so we followed his advice. Everyone else was going down, we alone were going up; and, incredibly, there was an exit on the eighth floor. The car park was built against the side of a hill and the eighth floor provided an exit to the top of the hill.

The obvious way out was down, but we had someone with us who knew another way, a better way. Life is full of frustration and difficulties, and men and women are always looking for answers, but these only take us deeper into the mire. But there is another way. Christ is the answer. He is the way of escape from life's mess.

Jesus is not only the way to God, he is the only way. He himself said that in life there are only two roads or ways. One is broad and very popular; many people are on it. The problem is that it leads to destruction. The other is narrow and it leads to life and God, but, sadly, few find it.

Just as in the multi-storey car park, most were going on what they considered to be the obvious way, but a few knew of another way. It seemed contrary to reason and certainly was not popular, but it was the right way.

Which way are you on?

8: More than Forgiveness

Salvation is more than forgiveness of sin. Thank God there is forgiveness for guilty sinners; but the gospel offers us more than that.

It is not unusual from time to time to hear that the ruler of a country on some great national occasion offers an amnesty to certain convicted criminals. Their sentences are reduced and they are set free. That is not an everyday occurrence but it is not unheard of. But what is never heard of is that the Queen, after granting the amnesty, should then stand at the gates of the gaol to welcome the forgiven criminals as they come to freedom — and then tell them that, as well as granting them freedom, she now wants them to come and live at Buckingham Palace, where she will treat them like one of the family. The love and care she shows to Charles, Anne, Andrew and Edward she will now show to them.

That is unheard of and is so impossible that it seems ridiculous even to think of it. But that is exactly what God does when he saves guilty sinners. He pardons all their sin — past, present and future — but more than that, he adopts them into his family. He makes them joint heirs with Christ of all the riches of heaven. He becomes their Father and they, because of adoption, are able to call him Father.

That is the glorious salvation that we have in the Lord Jesus Christ. It is far, far more than forgiveness.

9: Motorway Breakdown

Can you imagine a man happily driving down the M4 in his car? Then the car begins to shudder and splutter, loses power and eventually comes to a halt on the hard shoulder. He gets out, looks at his car and deduces that something is wrong. He is no mechanic, but he knows that much. But what is wrong?

He immediately sees something wrong. The wind-

screen is filthy, covered with the splattered remains of thousands of dead flies. This is something he can cope with, so he gets out his little yellow duster and soon has the windscreen sparkling clean. He has put right something that was wrong, so expectantly he tries the ignition key again, but the car still will not start.

Again he inspects his vehicle and sees something else wrong. One of the tyres is obviously under-inflated. He consults his handbook, checks the pressure in each tyre and brings the pressure in each up to the manufacturer's specification. He has put right something else that was wrong and again tries the ignition key, but still the car won't start.

You may think that is the silliest illustration you have ever heard. No-one would be so stupid as that. Maybe, but that is exactly how many people act with regard to seeking to make their lives acceptable to God. They realize there is something wrong, something missing in their lives. So they try to rectify it in all sorts of ways. They try morality, culture, education, even religion. That is as foolish as our friend on the M4 with his yellow duster and foot pump. What is wrong with his car is that there is no power in the engine. It is lifeless. And what is wrong with us cannot be put right by any self-effort. We are dead in sin and need the life that comes only from the Lord Jesus Christ.

The advice we would give to the motorist is to get on the 'phone and call the breakdown service — to get some help because the job is beyond his capabilities. And the advice we would give to every sinner is to get on your knees and call on Christ to save you. The job is beyond your efforts, but Jesus is able and willing to save all who call on him.

10: No Tie

Some restaurants like to maintain a certain standard on their premises and they refuse to allow a man in if he is not wearing a tie. Potential customers may not like this, but the owners of the restaurant have a perfect right to insist on their standards being met. But they are businessmen and they do not wish to turn customers away, so the waiter who initially refuses admission to a tieless man will then say, 'Do not go away, Sir', and he will provide a tie for the man. Once this is provided and put on, the standard is met and there is no barrier to admission.

The restaurant has set its standard for admission, but then provides its own answer for those who do not meet the standard.

God has set the standard for all who would come into

his presence. The standard is righteousness. God says that no-one who sins in any way will be allowed into heaven. That effectively bars us all, for there is not one righteous person. We all fail to meet God's standard. But in the gospel God tells us that he has met his own requirement for us, and provides a righteousness for us in Christ. 'This righteousness from God comes through faith in Jesus Christ to all who believe' (Rom. 3:22).

Contrary to the popular misconception, the prime purpose of the gospel is not to make sinners happy, but to make them righteous. You can be happy and go to hell, but if you have the righteousness of Christ, you are acceptable in heaven. To know this is true happiness.

11: The Robe of Righteousness

There is a tendency in us all to think that at the last count our good deeds will somehow prove acceptable to God. Isaiah shatters that illusion when he pronounces that 'all our righteous acts are like filthy rags' in the sight of God (Isa. 64:6). But the Old Testament prophet does not leave us in that depressing, though very real, dilemma. He also says that God 'has clothed me with garments of salvation and arrayed me in a robe of righteousness' (Isa. 61:10). This is a vivid illustration of how God provides forgiveness for guilty sinners who could never have done anything worthy of salvation.

A man comes home from work and tells his wife the good news that he has had promotion. To celebrate he is going to take his wife to the most expensive restaurant in town, a place they have never been before. 'We cannot go there,' she says, 'I've nothing to wear.' He fumes, thinking of the bulging wardrobes upstairs and all the cheques he has written for the dress shops. 'No!' she says. 'I know I have plenty of clothes, but nothing good enough for that place. If we are going there, I want to be presentable.'

Are you presentable for God? Do you think your morality and religion are good enough?

If you are not a Christian, let me tell you something about Christians. There was a time when none of us were Christians. We walked around in the robe of our own self-righteousness. We were proud of it — my efforts, my goodness, my achievements. I was as good as anyone. Who could tell me I was a sinner and not good enough for God? The robe of self-righteousness fitted well and we loved it, until God showed us the perfect, sinless purity of Jesus, and then we felt a bit tatty. Then, to make matters

[23]

worse, God said that all our best efforts were like filthy rags to him, and we felt dirty, guilty and vile.

The Bible calls this conviction of sin. We did not understand it at first, but oh, how we felt it!

What could we do? The obvious thing was to get another robe, another covering. We tried the garment of morality, and we stopped swearing and drinking and things like that. It worked all right for a while, until God showed us the real demands of his holy law. Then, like the robe of self-righteousness, it became transparent and useless.

So we tried the robe of religion. We went to church more often, put more money in the collection and became very religious. That too was all right for a while, until God showed us the cross, with his Son dying, bearing the punishment and guilt of sinners. Religion then became pathetic compared to that.

Conviction of sin came back and we really had no idea how to cope with it. Then God said, 'I will deal with your sin and give you a garment of salvation and a robe of righteousness.'

We came rather fearfully, but there was no need to fear because we found a God of amazing grace and deep love. He took us to his wardrobe of sovereign grace and brought out this most beautiful garment. We saw the price tag — purchased by the blood of Jesus. Amazingly, it had our name on it already. The Holy Spirit fitted it and there was no need for alteration. The fit was perfect.

Do you want this garment? Romans 3:22 tells us, 'This righteousness from God comes through faith in Jesus Christ to all who believe'. The only thing that can make us acceptable to God is that our righteousness be as good as God's — and God gives us this in the Lord Jesus Christ. When we come in repentance and faith to Jesus,

God credits us with the righteousness of his Son. His righteousness becomes ours and we are acceptable to God in Christ.

> *Accepted in the Well-beloved*
> *And clothed in righteousness divine,*
> *I see the bar to heaven removed,*
> *And all thy merits, Lord, are mine.*
> *Death, hell, and sin are now subdued;*
> *All grace is now to sinners given;*
> *And lo, I plead the atoning blood,*
> *And in thy right, I claim thy heaven.*

Charles Wesley

12: The Blood

Man's greatest need is righteousness and in the gospel God gives us the righteousness of Christ. This comes to us through faith, says Paul in Romans 3:22, and then in verse 25 he tells us something more particular about this saving faith — it is faith in his (Christ's) blood.

Blood is one of the most oft-repeated illustrations used in the Bible, and perhaps the most powerful. It will be impossible to understand the gospel if we do not understand why the Bible uses the word 'blood' to describe the death of Jesus. The Old Testament writers graphically describe blood sacrifices and their New Testament colleagues give these symbolic rituals a theological interpretation. They quite deliberately choose to use the word 'blood' three times more often than the 'cross' of Jesus, and five times more often than the 'death' of Jesus. Why?

The blood refers not only to the death of Jesus but to his sacrificial death. It tells us that the Saviour's death was a fulfilment of the Old Testament rituals. It was an atoning death. That is perfectly true, but there is more truth in this very special Bible illustration of the blood.

Leviticus 17:11 says that the life of the flesh is in the blood. So the blood not only speaks of death but also of life. Blood poured out would mean the end of life, and there is unquestionably this emphasis in the New Testament, but it does not end there. Jesus died on the cross as an atonement for our sins. His blood was shed in order that we who were dead in sin might have life. His blood means life for us. Our life is in his blood, and in that alone.

God chose to use the word and illustration of blood because there is no life without it. A person can live a day or two without water, and several weeks without food, but only a few minutes without oxygen — and oxygen is carried to the one hundred trillion cells in the body by blood.

Each cell in the human body depends for life upon the blood. Connecting all the cells together is an amazing system of blood vessels — sixty thousand miles of blood vessels in each body. Some are so small that they have a diameter of one-tenth of that of a human hair. Through the blood to the cells goes an endless supply of oxygen and everything else needed to maintain human life. Each cell in everybody lives at the mercy of the blood. No blood means no life. The heart is the pump that keeps the blood circulating.

This is how God has made us — dependent for life upon the blood. But man is more than a collection of a hundred trillion cells. He is a living soul made in the image of God; made to know and enjoy God. Sin has broken that image and brought spiritual death to everyone. What is the answer to spiritual death? It must be spiritual life, and this life comes to us only through the blood of Christ. This is God's way of salvation. Blood means death for Jesus, but life for us.

Faith in Christ's blood means faith in what he has done on the cross to deal with our sin. The blood of Christ deals with our sin by cleansing us from sin's effects (1 John 1:7). Blood-cleansing seems to be contrary to experience. If you get blood on your clothes, it stains not cleanses. So why does the Bible say that the blood cleanses from sin? Does the illustration fail at this point? No.

The blood carries to each cell of the body an endless supply of oxygen, nitrogen, sodium, calcium and everything else needed to maintain life. But our amazing God has also designed the body so that at the same time that the blood brings life-giving elements, it also absorbs the body's waste products — carbon dioxide, urea, uric acids — and the red cells deliver these waste chemicals to the organs that expel them from the body. The blood gives life and also sustains it by taking away the chemical by-products that would interfere with life — in other words, by cleansing.

Our human nature, polluted by sin, is always producing poisons like pride, lust, gossip and envy. These hinder any true relationship with God. They need to be got rid of and there is only one way — the blood of Christ. If sin is the great separator from God, then Jesus is the great reconciler. He brings us back to God. How? 'But now in Christ Jesus you who once were far away have been brought near through the blood of Christ' (Eph. 2:13).

The only way a sinner can come near to God is through the blood of Jesus — that is, through his death on the cross, which provides spiritual life for those dead in sin, and through the on-going cleansing blood that deals daily with our sin. John the Baptist said, 'Look, the Lamb of God, who takes away the sin of the world!' (John 1:29).

Has he taken your sin away?

Do you have faith in his blood? Faith in all that the Saviour has done for sinners?

(I am indebted to *In His Image* by Paul Brand and Philip Yancey for the technical details in this chapter.)

13: God's Workmanship

How do we become Christians? The popular notion is that we do so by trying our best. Salvation is therefore a reward for our efforts. The Bible says, 'No, this is not true.' Salvation is not the result of our works (Eph. 2:8-9), it is the result of God's work. The Christian is God's workmanship (Eph. 2:10).

This simple illustration tells us so much we need to know about salvation. A workman needs three things — raw material to work from, tools to work with and a design to work to.

I knew a man who was highly skilled and clever. He could do almost anything with a piece of wood, and his shed was full of all sorts of bits and pieces that he would never throw away because they might come in handy one day. There was one beautiful piece of teak that he always said he was keeping for a special job. It was so much better than the other wood he had and too good for most

jobs. So with this workman, as with most, his raw material varied. Some was excellent, some not so good.

God's raw material has no special pieces. It is all rubbish. The raw material of human nature is so twisted and warped by sin, so full of flaws and knots that it would take a workman of infinite skill to do anything with it. God is such a workman. There is no raw material that God cannot fashion into a thing of beauty. That truth gives every sinner hope.

As God begins to work on this raw material, his main tool is Scripture. As the Word is preached, the Holy Spirit begins the vital work of conviction. The hammer of God's law, the screwdriver of conviction and the plane of divine mercy to take off the rough edges, all do their work. Another tool is circumstance. A sickness, a chance meeting, an unexpected happening can all be used to show the sinner his need of salvation.

[29]

The design that God is working to is to make us like Jesus — to change our vile nature so that we radiate something of the beauty of Jesus. Only God can do this. Only God can make a Christian.

A Christian is not a patched-up sinner, he is a new creation. God does something in him so wonderful that the change cannot be explained in any other terms than that this person is God's workmanship.

14: No Visa

My wife and I were looking forward to our trip to Australia. We had been at Heathrow airport for several hours booking in and now we were in the boarding lounge. In a short time we would board the jumbo jet and our flight would begin.

There were four hundred people just like us in the boarding lounge, all excited and anticipating the journey. But one young lady about twenty years of age looked distressed. The airline staff kept coming back and forth to her. Questions were being asked and checks made. Eventually, the young lady was led away in tears.

The problem was that she had no visa. She wanted to go to Australia. She had bought her ticket and come expectantly to the airport, but she was not allowed to depart because she had no visa.

The visa is the official permission that the Australian government gives for foreigners to visit their land. It costs nothing and is very easily applied for through the Australian Consulate in this country. When the young lady bought her ticket, she would have been told that it is essential to apply for a visa. She had not done this and so was not allowed to board the plane. Perhaps she had forgotten. Perhaps she had been too busy to apply. Perhaps she had not taken the instruction seriously. Whatever the reason, she never got to the place to which she wanted to go.

Most people want to go to heaven. God, in the Bible, says he would be very happy for us to go there. He takes no pleasure in men and women going to hell, and he sent Jesus into this world to make it possible for us to go to heaven. But to guarantee us an entrance into heaven, we need a visa. Like the Australian visa, it costs us nothing and is very easy to apply for, but it is essential. There will be no entry without it.

This visa the Bible calls salvation. This salvation means that God forgives us all our sin. He saves us from what would have been the consequence of sin, namely hell, and makes us qualified for heaven and acceptable to him in the Lord Jesus Christ. Whatever else we may or may not have, if we are not saved we will never get to heaven.

But what if a man goes to church regularly, lives a good life and tries to be kind and considerate, will he be barred from entering heaven just because he is not saved? The Bible's answer to that is very clear. We only get into heaven because of Christ's righteousness, not our own. Our efforts are not good enough, therefore we must be saved. Are you?

Apply now, by going to Jesus in repentance and faith. Confess your sin to him and ask for forgiveness.

15: Halley's Comet

Halley's Comet orbits the sun about once every 76 years, which means that this remarkable sight can only be seen from earth every 76 years. The last time it could be seen was in 1986, and for several reasons the best place to see it was in the southern hemisphere.

From February to April 1986 I was in Australia, and so I was in the best place to see the comet. At the end of March I was preaching in a church in the north of New South Wales where there was a man who was very enthusiastic about Halley's Comet, and he was keen that I should see it. He gave me a drawing of the night sky with all the stars marked and showed me exactly where to look to see this visitor in the sky.

So not only was I in the best place to see the comet, but I had a friend who was pointing me in the right direction and providing every means for me to see this once-in-alifetime phenomenon. There was only one problem — I had to get up at four o'clock in the morning to see it. This did not appeal to me but I thought, 'I will never have the opportunity again', so up I got. I still do not know if I saw Halley's Comet. If I did, it was a great disappointment because it was nothing like as spectacular as I had anticipated.

There is another visitor from outside this world whom it is very important that you see. That visitor is Jesus. He came from heaven to seek and save those lost in sin. It is most probable that you are in the best place in the world to see him. By that, I mean that you can read the English language and therefore have access to the Bible in your language and a wealth of Christian books that tell you of Jesus. You live in a land where it is possible to hear the gospel preached, and faith in Jesus comes not through literally seeing him, but through hearing the gospel. It may well be that you have a friend who is very keen for you to become a Christian and has given you this little book.

All this is a great advantage, but it is not enough. If you are to become a Christian, you yourself must look to Jesus. No-one can do this for you, but if you truly look to him, you will not be disappointed and neither will you have any doubt at all that you have met with him.

To look to Jesus means to believe who he is and to trust him to deal with your sin and make you acceptable to God. Charles Spurgeon was the greatest preacher of the nineteenth century. He was saved as he heard a sermon preached on a verse in Isaiah, 'Look unto me and be ye saved.' As Spurgeon himself later described it, from the pulpit the preacher addressed him — ' "Young man, look to Jesus Christ. Look! Look! Look! You have nothin' to do but to look and live". I saw at once the way to salvation. I know not what else he said — I did not take much notice of it — I was so possessed with that one thought. Like as when the brazen serpent was lifted up, the people only looked and were healed, so it was for me. I had been waiting to do fifty things, but when I heard that word, "Look!" what a charming word it seemed to me! Oh! I looked until I could almost have looked my eyes away. There and then the cloud was gone, the darkness had rolled away, and that moment I saw the sun; and I could have risen that instant, and sung with the most enthusiastic of them, of the precious blood of Christ, and the simple faith which looks alone to Him. Oh, that somebody had told me this before, "Trust Christ, and you shall be saved".

'Yes, I had looked to Jesus as I was, and found in Him my Saviour. Thus had the eternal purpose of Jehovah decreed it; and as, the moment before, there was none more wretched than I was, so within the second, there was none more joyous. It took no longer time than does the lightning flash; it was done, and never has it been undone. I looked and lived, and leaped in joyful liberty as I beheld my sin punished upon the great Substitute, and put away for ever. I looked unto Him, as He bled upon that tree; His eyes darted a glance of love unutterable into my spirit, and in a moment, I was saved.

'The frown of God no longer resteth upon me; but my Father smiles, I see His eyes — they are glancing love; I hear His voice — it is full of sweetness. I am forgiven, I am forgiven, I am forgiven!'

The details of all conversion experiences are not exactly like Spurgeon's, but nobody becomes a Christian unless he looks to Jesus. He alone can forgive your sin, so look to him, trust him, ask him to be your Saviour. Look and live!

16: The Statue

Cwmbran is the only new town in Wales. In the early years of its development the authorities decided to commission a statue to stand in the shopping centre, depicting a family in the new town, of father, mother and child.

One day the statue appeared in its designated spot, all boarded up, awaiting the official unveiling ceremony. People were naturally curious to see what it looked like. Then the great day came and the statue was unveiled. People gasped with amazement at what they saw. The following comments were actually heard:

'What is it?'

'It looks like three drunken worms.'

'It looks better with the boards up.'

The statue caused a great commotion. TV crews came to see and record. The papers interviewed people for their opinion on the statue and everyone had a view to express.

[35]

What caused the stir was that the statue was in the style of modern art, and very few people liked or understood it. If it had been a conventional statue, no-one would have given it a second look. It was the difference that caused people to sit up and take notice.

The Christians in the Acts of the Apostles caused a stir everywhere they went because they were different. Their lives, actions, ambitions and beliefs were different, and people took note of them. Today we try desperately to make our faith acceptable to people by making our Christianity no different from their life-style. So Christians go to the pub after church for a drink; Christians laugh at the world's unsavoury jokes; Christians delight in the world's ungodly music. We are desperately trying to show them that really we are exactly like them.

The result is that the church has no effect upon the world. The world ignores us. Why should it bother if we are no different? But the Bible calls upon us to be different; and this difference can be a very important means of evangelism. How often have you heard a testimony of salvation in which the person says that what first attracted him to Christianity was a friend who 'had something that I did not have'?

But apart from evangelism, the difference is something that God commands for his own glory. Listen to how Paul so clearly spells this out for the Ephesians:

'So I tell you this, and insist on it in the Lord, that you must no longer live as the Gentiles do, in the futility of their thinking' (4:17).

'For you were once darkness, but now you are light in the Lord. Live as children of light (for the fruit of the light consists in all goodness, righteousness and truth) and find out what pleases the Lord. Have nothing to do with the fruitless deeds of darkness, but rather expose them' (5:8-11).

17: Jack the Giant Killer

My grandson Jonathan, like all three- or four-year-old children, loves to be told stories. He could sit and listen for hours to all the well-loved old fairy stories and the ones made up especially for him. But if he were to be asked which story he wanted first, the answer would always be, 'Jack the Giant Killer'.

So when the school took all the four-year-olds to see the pantomime, 'Jack the Giant Killer', he was very excited. He sat in the theatre next to his mother enjoying the colour and fun of the occasion. All was well until the giant appeared on stage; then he literally jumped from his seat onto his mother's lap in fear.

He could listen all day to the story of the giant. He knew the details by heart. But when confronted with the 'real' thing, he was afraid.

Isn't that like many Christians? We all have to face what seem to us to be giants in our life — problems, weaknesses, sins that seem too great for us to cope with. We can talk to Christian friends about them and listen to sermons on how to deal with them, but when they actually confront us we are terrified and the 'giant' triumphs yet again in our lives.

How can we become spiritual giant-killers? Do you remember the story of David and Goliath in 1 Samuel 17? The giant was very confident in his defiance of God's people. 'This day I defy the ranks of Israel! Give me a man and let us fight each other', he said (v.10). No-one would take up the challenge because they were all afraid. The size of Goliath terrified them.

The giants of today still shout their challenges at God's people. We all know them and, sadly, we often feel totally inadequate and retreat in fear. What should we do? Follow the example of David.

No-one gave David a chance against the giant, but he himself was confident. This confidence was not the silly arrogance of youth, but was based on one thing only. This giant was defying God, so David faced the enemy in the name of God, confident that the battle is the Lord's.

Everyone knows the result.

What giants are you facing? Fear of witnessing? Prayerlessness? Are you resigned to failure? Then remember David and believe that the battle is the Lord's. Face the giant with faith and courage. Trust God as David did and expect to see the giants fall.

18: Fear

A Christian said to me, 'Pastor, why can't I pray in the prayer meeting?' He was voicing his despair at the fear that prevented him from opening his mouth in a prayer meeting. He wanted to pray but fear of man, fear of his limitation, prevented him. A Christian lady said to me, 'Pastor, every time I am about to pray, you close the prayer meeting.' As we talked about this, she agreed with me that if the prayer meeting went on for another hour she would always be just about to pray when I closed it. In other words it was the same problem of fear keeping her silent when she wanted to pray.

This is a real problem for most Christians — fear of praying publicly, fear of witnessing, in spite of the fact that they love the Lord and want to do these things.

In Judges 6, we see that Gideon was a man riddled with fears:

v.11: He was afraid of the Midianites.

v.15: He had no confidence in his own ability.

vv.22-23: He was afraid of God in a wrong way.

v.27: He was afraid of his family.

In Judges 7:3, God tells Gideon that all in the army who were fearful were to go home. Twenty-two thousand fearful men left, but Gideon did not. On the evidence of chapter 6, you would think Gideon would have been the first to leave.

The lesson is clear. There is a fear that God will use and there is a fear that God will not use. The difference is that one fear renders us totally incapable, but the other fear causes us to be thrown in complete dependence upon the Lord's strength. Fear is not wrong, it only becomes wrong when it causes us to forget that our strength comes always from the Lord.

To the man who could not pray in the prayer meeting I said, 'You can do it. Do it next time.' He did, and conquered his fear. To the lady I said, 'Pray first in the next prayer meeting.' She did, and by the grace of God she prayed in spite of her fear.

It does not always work out so well in dealing with the fears that Christians have, but there is no reason why it should not. Do not let fear render you helpless. Remember Gideon, and trust the Lord.

19: The Blitz

During 1941 London was bombed night after night by German planes. This bombing was known as the Blitz. Thousands were killed and whole areas of the city completely destroyed. It was a frightening time to live in

England's capital city. Yet only 200 miles away in Paris no bombs were falling.

Why was London being blitzed and Paris not? The simple answer is that Hitler and his German army had already captured Paris. The French capital was no threat to him, hence no bombs. But London was a free city and very much opposed to Hitler. London was blitzed because it was at war with Hitler.

The Christian is at war with Satan and all the power of evil, so it is not surprising that Satan bombards us with all sorts of temptations and troubles. These are evidence of the war and proof that we no longer belong to Satan. We are free in the Lord Jesus Christ. Salvation has liberated us from the bondage of sin, and Satan does not like it. He cannot rob us of our salvation — that is secure in Christ — but he can make life uncomfortable for the believers. So when the battle gets hot, do not lose heart; just praise God that you are in the fight and not still in spiritual bondage.

Everyone in the village knew Will and how faithful he was to the chapel. One Sunday as he was walking as usual to chapel, two of the lads of the village offered him a lift in their car. Will gratefully accepted. As they were driving along, one of the lads asked the old saint, 'Will, if the Devil was to stand in the middle of the road and stop the car, who would he go for first, you or us?' Will answered, 'Me boys — he's got you already.'

20: A Heart Attack

In August 1985 I was at the Evangelical Movement of Wales Conference in Aberystwyth. On the Tuesday afternoon I was preaching at an open-air meeting on the prom. I spoke of the two questions we usually ask a friend we meet unexpectedly on holiday — 'How long are you staying?' and 'When are you going home?' I applied these evangelistically and asked the crowd, 'How long are you staying in this world? Have you got a home in heaven?' I said that, as a Christian, if I were to die today, I would go to my home in heaven. I preached along these lines for about fifteen minutes.

When I had finished, I stood in the crowd as the service continued. Ten minutes later I had a heart attack. I spent the next week in hospital and, while there, had many cards from friends assuring me of their prayers. But one friend who had been at the open-air meeting wrote, 'Peter, there is no need to make your sermon illustrations so dramatic!' What he meant was that I was speaking about 'If I died today' — and then had a heart attack.

As I lay in hospital, I thought about this. Do we really believe what we say we do? It is easy to make great sounding statements when everything is O.K., but when things suddenly go wrong, do we still believe them? Are we fair-weather Christians?

Thank God that he upholds us in our weaknesses and somehow makes his love more precious than ever. Yes, I did believe what I had preached. I had a home to go to — but not yet. In that hospital bed God showed me the greatness of his love in a very wonderful way. I came across a hymn by William Williams that I had never seen before:

> *To see Thy face, Beloved, makes my poor soul rejoice*
> *O'er all I've ever tasted, or ever made my choice.*
> *When they all disappear, why should I grieve or pine*
> *While to my gaze there opens the sight that Christ is mine?*
>
> *He's greater than His blessings, He's greater than His*
> *grace,*
> *Far greater than His actions, whatever you may trace;*
> *I'll plead for faith, gifts, cleansing: for these I'll yearn*
> *quite sore,*
> *But on Him only, always, I'll look and lean far more.*

Outside of Scripture, I do not think any words had ever spoken to me so powerfully and meaningfully as these by William Williams. The wonderful love of God thrilled my heart and mind afresh. What fools we are to let anything cloud the reality of God's grace and mercy! Some more words by Williams came to my mind:

> *Jesus, Jesus, all sufficient,*
> *Beyond telling is Thy worth;*
> *In Thy Name lie greater treasures*
> *Than the richest found on earth.*
> *Such abundance is my portion with my God.*

Is there anything in this world more wonderful than having a living experience of the Lord Jesus Christ?

[42]

21: Ruined

When I was a student in college, I spent two summers working for a local council, cutting grass in a cemetery. The man in charge of the cemetery had a strange aversion to anything Christian and lost no opportunity to attack my Christian faith.

One day as we were working together, he pointed to a man walking through the cemetery and said, 'There's a man who was ruined by Christianity.' He went on to explain that during the Second World War that man was deeply involved in the local 'black market'. In the war years everyone had ration books; everything was in short supply and certain goods were virtually impossible to obtain. But the 'black market' men could get you any-thing — at a highly-inflated price. I was told that this man was making a fortune selling goods on the 'black market'.

'He was raking it in,' said my foreman, 'but then he got converted and gave it all up. Christianity ruined him.'

What a marvellous, even though unintentional, testi-mony to the power of the gospel! Paul says that when we become Christians, we become new creatures; old things pass away, all things become new. Christianity ruins us for dishonesty and greed. It breaks the power of sin. Christ gives us a new life with new ambitions, new desires, new standards. It ruins us for sin.

22: Revival

'Will you not revive us again, that your people may rejoice in you? . . . that his glory may dwell in our land' (Psa. 85:6,9).

Revival implies life. The psalmist asks that God should revive us, the people of God. God does not revive the dead; what they need is regeneration. Imagine a man pulled unconscious out of the sea. His rescuers will try to revive him by giving him the kiss of life. But if he has been in the sea for several days, no-one will try to revive him. It would be impossible.

So it is with spiritual revival. It is impossible to revive the spiritually dead. They need regeneration. In other words, revival is a work of God among believers, those who are already alive in Christ but whose life has waned and weakened. They have lost all sense of the joy of the Lord. Sin cannot rob them of their salvation, but it can certainly render them useless in the service of God. Such Christians need reviving.

Initially, revival is not the answer to a godless society. It is the answer to a lifeless, powerless church. A revived church filled with the power of the Spirit is the answer to a godless society. 'Revive *us*', says the psalmist, 'that your people may rejoice in you. *Then* we will see glory again in our land.'

James Buchanan's definition of revival makes this clear:

'Revival properly consists in two things: A general impartation of new life, vigour and power to those who are already of the number of God's people, and a remarkable awakening and conversion of souls who have hitherto been careless and unbelieving.'

In other words it consists in new spiritual life imparted to the dead and new spiritual health imparted to the living.

23: Frozen Food

Our churches are, sometimes, very much like frozen food — cold, unattractive and unyielding, more at home in a fridge than anywhere else. But once let the heat get to the frozen food, and everything changes. The coldness disappears, the unattractive becomes appetizing, and the stiff and rigid becomes flexible and usable.

How we need the fire of God in our churches. By 'fire' we do not mean noise and nonsense but the warmth and passion of the Holy Spirit.

We need the fire of Mount Sinai, which brought before the people the sense of the holiness of God and the obedience he expected from them.

We need the fire of Carmel, where God vindicated his own name and false religion was blasted before the glory and power of the only true God.

We need the fire of Pentecost, which resulted in thousands being saved.

Nearly five hundred times in Scripture, fire is used as a symbol of the presence of God. John the Baptist promised that Jesus would baptize his people with fire. The old Methodist, Samuel Chadwick, said, 'The supreme need of the church is fire. The baptism of the Spirit is the baptism of fire. Spirit-filled souls are ablaze for God. They love with a love that glows. They believe with a faith that kindles. They serve with a devotion that consumes. They hate sin with a fierceness that burns.'

Who can deny our need today for this fire?

24: The Tatty Old Sleeve

The story is told of a country church in Wales during the 1859 revival. On a particular Sunday, they had no recognized preacher in the pulpit. Great things were happening in the land and thousands were coming to faith in Christ, but on this Sunday no-one was expecting much blessing. In the prayer meeting before the service one man prayed, 'Lord, you know we have no great preacher here today.' He went on to describe some preachers as like a beautiful suit of clothes, but their preacher that day was just a tatty old sleeve.

To everyone's surprise, the preacher was mightily used by God and many were saved. It was recognized that though the preacher was only a tatty old sleeve, God's arm had filled the sleeve and great blessing flowed.

Maybe your pastor is not much of a preacher. Perhaps you are tempted to talk rather disparagingly about his ministry, but remember the tatty old sleeve and what God can do. Pray that God's arm will fill the sleeve in your church. The man God used in a most remarkable way in Wales during the 1859 revival was a Presbyterian minister named David Morgan. He had exercised a very ordinary ministry for a number of years, but he said that one night he went to bed like a lamb and woke up like a lion. The power of the Holy Spirit had come upon him.

Pray earnestly for your minister that the same God-given power may come upon his preaching.

25:
Picking
Apples

During the first twenty years of our married life we lived in four different houses. They were nice enough places, but not one had much of a garden. So it was a real joy to move into our fifth house, which not only had a nice garden, but also three mature apple trees.

The first autumn saw a magnificent crop of apples and we were determined to save as many as possible. So after they were picked, we wrapped each one separately in newspaper and stacked them on wooden trays in the garage. We looked forward with anticipation to apples all the winter. By Christmas they were all rotten.

I spoke to a farmer friend about this and he said it was because I had picked them too soon. I protested that they looked ripe. Yes, he said, but did they come easily? He explained that the right time to pick apples is when they come away from the branch easily into your hand. 'If you have to tug, leave them', he said. 'They are not ready for picking and will go rotten.'

[48]

That was good advice on picking apples, but it is also good advice on dealing with the souls of men and women. How often in our churches have we been overjoyed to see people make a profession of faith, but within a short time it is obvious that they are are not saved and soon they stop attending church. This is so dishonouring to God. Also it is a cause of deep disappointment and frustration for us Christians, and it very often makes those who made the profession very hardened against the gospel. They say, 'I was saved — and it does not work.'

It is a very real problem. The modern 'invitation system' aggravates it, but even in churches who do not use this system and where more care is taken in dealing with souls, it still happens. Why is this so? Often, like me with the apples, it is ignorance coupled with enthusiasm. We are so eager to see souls saved that we ignore basic biblical principles. As a consequence of this, we hurry souls to a decision before they are ready. How can we know when the right time has arrived to pick spiritual fruit?

Firstly, we must always remember that a true conversion is not the result of human decision but a work of the Holy Spirit. There are evidences of this divine work. We read in Acts 11:23 that at Antioch Barnabas saw the evidence of the grace of God. The prime evidence is always conviction of sin, which will lead to repentance. There can be no salvation without this. Conviction will vary in degree from one person to another, but it must be there.

In past generations Christians used to make a distinction between a soul awakened and a soul saved. By 'awakened' they meant that the Holy Spirit was beginning to deal with the person. Conviction was coming and a longing for pardon was being created. But this was not yet conversion. Perhaps we today ought again to make this distinction and not try to hasten the work which the Holy Spirit is beginning.

This does not mean that we sit back and do nothing. If you see souls that God is awakening, then pray for them. Help and advise, but let the Holy Spirit do his own peculiar work. When they are ripe, they will come easily and no pressure will be needed. There are no rotten apples in a harvest that is reaped by the Holy Spirit of God.

26: Children and Church

When our eldest daughter was fifteen, she hated going to church. Every Sunday was a battle. She was embarrassed that her father was a minister and in her rebellion declared herself to be an atheist. We did not have this difficulty with our two other children, but this was a real problem. We insisted that she attend church, even though it was obvious that she never listened. Then one Sunday evening after going through the usual arguments before getting her to church, the Holy Spirit broke into her life in glorious saving power. There was no prior indication of any spiritual work in her, and when I saw her in tears during the last hymn I did not think of conviction of sin, but assumed she was ill. Praise God it was conviction that led to deep repentance and a true work of grace that completely transformed her life.

I tell this story because the experience is all too common in Christians' homes. Many parents do not know how to cope with their children's spiritual rebellion and they give in. It is not unusual to see children of

Christian parents stop attending church at about eleven or twelve. Many parents are afraid of forcing their children to go to church in case this will cause resentment and an adverse reaction in later years. One can understand and sympathize with this fear, but it must not be allowed to deter the Christian parent from fulfilling the God-given responsibility for the spiritual well-being of the child. Parents must insist with firmness and love that the life which the Lord has given into their charge shall come under the sound of the Word of God.

God is sovereign in salvation. He can save whom he wills, when he wills, how he wills, but he has decreed that the prime means of salvation is the preaching of the gospel, and every time the gospel is preached there is the possibility of salvation. Do not deprive your children of the great privilege of hearing the Word of God.

27: Love and Law

Imagine a boy who throws a brick through the window of a Woolworths store, and then throws a brick through the window of his father's house.

His action in both cases is wilful and wrong, but the consequences will be different. Woolworths will send for the police and the law will be involved. The father won't send for the police. He will punish his son but he will not involve the law. Why not? Because this is his son, and though the boy's action grieves the father, he is still his son and is dealt with as such.

Romans 8:1 says there is no condemnation for those in Christ Jesus. This means that when we sin as Christians, this sin does not cause us to pick up the wages of sin, which is death. Why not? 'Because through Christ Jesus the law of the Spirit of life set me free from the law of sin and death' (Rom. 8:2). The law of sin and death condemns us. Sin is the breaking of God's law and this brings upon men divine wrath (Rom. 4:15). The law of the Spirit of life sets us free from this condemnation. It justifies us. It puts us into another category — we are now under grace, not under law (Rom. 6:14). So when as Christians we sin, the law is not called in to deal with us. If that were the case, we would be condemned. Instead, the grace and love of God deals with us. The Christian's sin deeply grieves God, and, make no mistake about it, he will chastise us; but he will never condemn us.

'No condemnation' does not mean that we get away with sin. The father does not let his son get away with throwing a brick through the window. He will punish him, perhaps by stopping his pocket money or withdrawing other favours. He deals with his son firmly, strictly even, but always in love because this is his son. The law would not be so gracious.

'No condemnation' does not mean that the Christian can take sin lightly. Romans 6 makes this clear. But it does mean that we can never lose our salvation. Nothing can separate us from the love of God that is in Christ Jesus our Lord (Rom. 8:38,39). We are 'in Christ' and he is our security.

28: Dead to Sin

Christians say sometimes when they have sinned, 'I could not help it. I tried not to do it, but the temptation was too great.'

How does this square with the teaching of Romans 6 that we are dead to sin and that the slavery of sin finished the moment we were saved? Quite simply, the above excuse cannot be justified biblically. Sin is no longer our master, therefore it cannot compel us to do anything. There is a difference between temptation and compulsion. To the temptation we can say 'yes' or 'no'. Compulsion does not give us that choice.

The Christian is not a slave to sin and therefore not under sin's compulsion. Sin can tempt us, but it cannot force us. We are in Christ and therefore dead to sin's slavery.

Imagine a slave in the first century. His master says, 'Slave, go there; do this; fetch that.' He is a slave and has no choice but to obey his master. Then the slave dies. The master stands over his dead body and says, 'Slave, go there; do this; fetch that,' but now there is no obedience. The slave is dead to the master's power.

The non-Christian is a slave to sin. His will is not free. Salvation sets the slave free and only then does his will become free. He can now say 'no' to sin and if he does not, it is not because he could not, but because he would not. No sin is excusable, but thank God it is all pardonable.

'Dead to sin' does not mean that we are dead to its influence, but it does mean that we are dead to its power. If we say we could not stop ourselves sinning, then we are saying that it is still our master. But it is not. The Christian is a servant of righteousness, not sin (Rom. 6:17,18).

Memorize 1 Corinthians 10:13: 'No temptation has seized you except what is common to man. And God is faithful; he will not let you be tempted beyond what you can bear. But when you are tempted, he will also provide a way out so that you can stand up under it.'

29: Sanctification

Salvation is like being pulled out of a raging sea when waves were about to engulf you. You have been saved and the waves cannot harm. You are safe — safe on the Rock, Christ Jesus.

But salvation is more than a rescue operation. You must go on to enjoy the life you were saved for. You are on the rock, and in front of you is a seemingly unclimbable steep cliff. You realize you could no more climb that yourself than you could have got out of the water yourself. Again, I stress, you are safe on the rock, but you want to go on and upward to the fuller life. The question is, how? Then you see a rope hanging down from the top of the cliff, and you hear a voice shouting instructions to you and saying, 'You climb, and I will pull.'

That is sanctification. You are to climb over all the seemingly impossible obstacles that would try to keep you down, and at the same time God is drawing you upward and onward.

There is no such thing as instant sanctification. It is not a once-and-for-all experience like justification, but a process. It begins at salvation and goes on for the rest of our lives. The Christian can grow in sanctification but he can also decline in it. How sanctified you are will depend upon how submissive and obedient you are to the will of God. As the above illustration shows, God is involved in our sanctification and all the strength and help that we need he will supply; but it does require a determined effort on our part.

In Romans 12:1 Paul urges us to offer our bodies as a living sacrifice to God. He has to urge us because, sadly, too many Christians are satisfied with being saved and show little concern to grow spiritually. Consequently, so many God-given gifts lie waste because of indifference and lack of commitment. We are to offer our bodies to God; this means all we are, our total being — heart, mind, will, hands, feet etc. The Bible never offers a compromise to Christians. It demands all we are and have.

Have you ever daydreamed about being a great preacher or a missionary reaching some unknown tribe with the gospel? Daydreaming is useless because it accomplishes nothing. You actually do nothing. God does not want our daydreams. He wants our bodies, and then perhaps our dreams will become realities. A disembodied sanctification is not biblical. Sanctification is the giving of ourselves totally to God. It means trusting him, obeying him, pleasing him and loving him with all our hearts. In other words, sanctification means being like the Lord Jesus Christ.

30: The Receipt

As any father would testify, when a daughter gets married it is a very expensive time. The reception, cars, flowers, plus a hundred-and-one other things, all have to be paid for, so it is a great relief when all the bills are met in full.

About a year after my daughter's wedding, we received a letter from the hotel where the reception had been held, stating that they had no record of my paying the bill for the reception. Panic! That was a big bill and there was no way I could pay it again. So the search began for the receipt. What a tremendous relief it was when I was able to produce the receipt which proved that my debt had been fully paid. Once the hotel manager saw this, there was no more argument. The matter was settled. The receipt proved it.

As sinners, we had a great debt. We had broken the law of God time and time again, but the great message of the gospel is that Jesus has paid that debt for us and the proof, the receipt, is the cross. Paul tells the Colossians that God 'forgave us all our sins, having cancelled the written code, with its regulations, that was against us and that stood opposed to us; he took it away, nailing it to the cross' (Col. 2:13,14). It is as if there is a great bill with our name on it which lists all our sins; but Jesus has taken that bill, paid it for us and nailed it to the cross, which is the equivalent of stamping it 'paid in full'.

As Christians, we still sin and Satan comes to us to accuse us and try to rob us of assurance. John Newton, the former slave dealer, who by the grace of God became a preacher of the gospel, must have known much of such accusations. With all his past as well as his present sin, Satan would tempt him to ask how he could be a Christian. Don't we all know something of this? But Newton knew how to answer Satan:

> *I may my fierce accuser face,*
> *And tell him thou hast died.*

He had the receipt of his salvation, namely the cross. When you are attacked like this, wave the receipt in the face of Satan. He has no answer to the blood of Jesus.

> *When Satan tempts me to despair,*
> *And tells me of the wrong within,*
> *Upward I look, and see him there*
> *Who made an end of all my sin.*

SILVERSTONES HOTEL

21 BALCOMBE ROAD
HAYWARDS HEATH SUSSEX

Wedding Reception held on February 22 1992:

Buffet lunch	250·00
Wedding cake	100·00
Cake stand and knife	15·00
Flowers	125·00
Use of room service	75·00
	£ 565·00

Received with thanks

[57]

31: A New Grand-daughter

My grand-daughter was two weeks old when I saw her for the first time. I thought she was the most beautiful baby in the world. Some might say, 'You are prejudiced'. Of course I am. She is part of me; one of the family; she belongs to us and she is precious. I do not expect others to see her as I do, but to me she is very special.

As a Christian, my relationship with Jesus makes him very special. Many people regard Jesus with respect, but polite indifference. They may see him as a great teacher, a remarkable moral leader or social reformer, but they would hardly say, 'Jesus is precious'. But this is how the Christian sees him. Jesus is the altogether lovely one. He is the fairest of ten thousand. 'He is', says the apostle Peter, 'precious to those who believe' (1 Pet. 2:7). And this is because of the special relationship that each Christian has with the Saviour. He is part of us; we belong to him and he belongs to us. There is a union between us that makes him precious indeed. We are biased towards Jesus because we love him.

The first night after we saw our grand-daughter, my wife woke up about 2 a.m. She woke me and I could see she was distressed. 'Where is the baby?', she said, 'Where is the baby?' She had had a bad dream and dreamt that we had lost the baby. The thought of losing someone so precious was frightening.

Christian, do you love Jesus like this? Would the thought of being separated from him cause you deep distress? Of course it would. To know him is to love him, and to love him is to love him above all things. Thank God that nothing can separate us from the love of God which is in Christ Jesus our Lord.

SOME OTHER
BANNER OF TRUTH
TITLES

STEPPING-STONES
A NEW TESTAMENT GUIDE FOR BEGINNERS
Peter Jeffery

A knowledge of the teaching of the New Testament is a vital part of spiritual growth. But to become familiar with its 27 books and their 260 chapters seems a daunting prospect for any new or young Christian. Where can we find help to begin? In *Stepping-Stones* Peter Jeffery provides exactly what we need. In a clear, understandable and interesting way he outlines the contents of each book in the New Testament and explains its main themes. *Stepping-Stones* meets a widely-felt need. It is an ideal introduction to the study of the New Testament and a valuable companion for Christians who want to grow in their understanding of the gospel.

Peter Jeffery is minister of Bethlehem Evangelical Church, Port Talbot, Wales.

ISBN 0 85151 597 5
144pp. Large paperback

RIGHT WITH GOD

John Blanchard

Right With God is a straightforward book to help those searching for a personal faith in God. It has been widely used throughout the English-speaking world and translated into many other languages. This latest edition is itself the tenth in English.

'This book is a prize indeed. John Blanchard uses his considerable powers of analysis to set out the great truths of the gospel in a way that is both clear and compelling. Thank God for it!' *The Rev J. A. Motyer, one-time Principal of Trinity College, Bristol.*

'John Blanchard writes as clearly as he speaks, so that misunderstanding is impossible. I do not know any book quite like it.' *The Rev R. C. Lucas, St. Helen's, Bishopsgate, London.*

'The best modern book we have seen for explaining the gospel to the serious non-Christian.' *Come.*

'Buy it, read it, and make use of it!' *The Evangelical Presbyterian.*

John Blanchard is an internationally-known evangelist and Bible teacher. A co-founder of Christian Ministries, *he is the author of 12 books and his other work includes radio and television broadcasting.*

ISBN 0 85151 045 0
128pp. Paperback

COME TO ME!
AN URGENT INVITATION TO TURN TO CHRIST

Tom Wells

'Come to me, all you who are weary and burdened, and I will give you rest. Take my yoke upon you and learn from me, for I am gentle and humble in heart, and you will find rest for your souls. For my yoke is easy and my burden is light.'

These are, perhaps, the best known and most frequently heard words which Jesus ever spoke. They are read at church services, funerals and many other occasions. They are often called 'the comfortable words'. But what do they mean? What does it mean to *'come'* to Jesus? Who is he, and why should we *'come'* to him?

In this attractive presentation of the Christian faith, Tom Wells answers these questions. In an engaging style he explains who Jesus Christ is and what it means to 'come' to him. He writes honestly about the barriers which stand in the way of faith, and about the cost involved in being a disciple. But he also shows clearly that there is nothing more important we can ever do than 'come' to Christ.

Tom Wells is a preacher and writer in Cincinnati, Ohio, U.S.A. He is also the author of Faith: The Gift of God; A Vision for Missions; Christian: Take Heart! *and* The Moral Basis of Faith, *all of which are published by the Banner of Truth.*

ISBN 08151 471 5
120pp. Paperback

FAITH: THE GIFT OF GOD

Tom Wells

Two men hear the Gospel. They are from similar backgrounds. One turns to faith in Christ; the other turns away from Christ. Why the difference? Faith in the one, unbelief in the other! But how does faith come? Answers vary considerably. Some lay emphasis on God's work; others stress man's action. Many imply that a doctrinal understanding of the problem does not matter.

In this book Tom Wells shows us that it certainly matters. He invites us (1) to search into the Scriptures which bear on the matter and (2) to look back and examine our own coming to faith in Christ. Under the blessing of the Holy Spirit this should help our whole understanding of the doctrines of God, man and salvation.

The conclusion that the faith with which we believe is only ours because God creates it in our heart arises from man's evil nature and God's holy character. No man left to himself will ever turn to Christ. Nor will God share his glory with another. Salvation is all of grace. Faith *is* the gift of God.

This book is a refreshingly new approach to a Biblical understanding of the doctrines of faith and salvation. It is an attempt 'to write theology for the ordinary man'.

ISBN 0 85151 361 1
160pp. Paperback

THE MYSTERY OF PROVIDENCE

John Flavel

Do we believe that everything in the world and in our own lives down to the minutest details is ordered by the providence of God? Do we ever take time to observe and meditate on the workings of providence? If not, are we missing much?

It should be a delight and pleasure to us to discern how God works all things in the world for his own glory and his people's good. But it should be an even greater pleasure to observe the particular designs of providence in our own lives. 'O what a world of rarities', says John Flavel, 'are to be found in providence . . . With what profound wisdom, infinite tenderness and incessant vigilance it has managed all that concerns us from first to last.' It was to persuade Christians of the excellency of observing and meditating upon this that Flavel first published his *Mystery of Providence* in 1678. Since then the work has gone through many editions. Based on the words 'God that performeth all things for me' (Psalm 57:2) this work shows us how providence works for us in every stage and experience of our lives. The book is richly illustrated from the lives of believers and from the author's wide reading in church history. There are avenues of spiritual knowledge and experience opened to the Christian in this work which he probably never knew existed.

ISBN 0 85151 104 X
224pp. Paperback